REDEEMED

*Extraordinary Grace
for Ordinary People*

AMY R. DUNHAM

REGULAR BAPTIST
RBP **Press**

Dedication

I couldn't do any of this without my husband. He encourages me, loves me, leads me, and forgives me. He works hard for me and our three girls, relentlessly giving himself in the office and at home. I am so happy that our girls will grow up with such a wonderful father who will help point them to their true and better Heavenly Father. I love you, Dan.

Redeemed: Extraordinary Grace for Ordinary People
© 2018 Regular Baptist Press • Arlington Heights, Illinois
www.RegularBaptistPress.org • 1-800-727-4440
Printed in U.S.A. All rights reserved.
RBP5514 • ISBN: 978-1-62940-950-4

Contents

Introduction

I didn't want to write about Ruth. When God began to whisper her name to me and point me to her story, I pushed it aside. It isn't the story I would choose to unpack with you. This tiny book squished between Judges and 1 Samuel seemed too common, too ordinary.

Is that too honest? Perhaps. But God is faithful and persistent. As I read each word again and again, I became acquainted with a woman who began to feel like a friend. It became clear that what I thought was just a simple, everyday story of a common woman was so much more.

Ruth was a Moabite, she was a widow, and she was poor. But God took notice and delighted in using this ordinary woman to birth a king and, eventually, the Messiah. This is no coincidence. This is how our Heavenly Father works, using both the grand and the ordinary, both the strong and the weak, both the sought-after and the looked-over, both a thundering earthquake and a still small voice.

Ruth's life not only provides insight into how to live out our own faith, but it paints a portrait of redemption and highlights a humble moment in the intricate landscape of the gospel story. In four short chapters we meet a woman with such faith, an aged widow of such grief, and a man of such love that we can't walk away unchanged. And we simply can't walk away without knowing more of our Redeemer and the grandeur of His passion for us.

It is my prayer that the richness of God's Word would be open to you and that the fullness of the gospel would be blindingly clear as we get to know Ruth. And that by knowing her story better, we will become better acquainted with the Son of God, Who humbled Himself, wrapped Himself in human flesh, left His glory, died, and rose again in order to bestow forgiveness upon us.

This is what it means to be redeemed.

How to Use This Study

Under the title of each lesson is the Bible reference for the passage covered in that lesson. Please read the entire passsage before you start the lesson. You will be asked to reread portions of the passage as you work your way through the lesson.

At the end of each lesson, you will be asked three questions: What does this tell me about God? Which of God's attributes is displayed in this passage? and How can I apply what I've learned to my life?

These three questions are fundamental to studying the Bible and will help you learn how to study on your own. Your answers may, and will most likely, be different from others' answers. That is okay! The Bible is God's Word. It is active—living and breathing—and God will speak to you personally through His Word if you are listening.

If you are unfamiliar with God's attributes or just like to have a handy reference nearby, like I do, I have included a list of key attributes with a brief description of each (p. 9). This will help you in answering the second of the three questions. The list by no means includes all of God's attributes.

Finally, throughout each lesson you will mainly see three types of questions. Some will be straightforward question-and-answer formats that will come right from the Biblical text. These questions are meant to send you back to the Bible to help you look strategically at what is being said.

Other questions will ask you to write out different passages. This is because writing out a verse or verses on paper begins to write the words on our memories as well. You may even want to memorize these passages.

Another type of question includes "What do you think?" These questions are the hardest for some, because we all want to have the right answer. However, these questions may not give

a right answer or may not have a right answer that we can de-
termine with the information given in the passage. I ask, "What
do you think?" because I want you to share what you think. You
may think your answer seems silly, that your answer's too personal, or that no one else thinks the way you do. That's great! At
least you are thinking.

Attributes of God

Eternal God always has been and always will be. He has no beginning and no end. He exists undiminished into the future. See Exodus 3:14 and Hebrews 13:8.

Good God is good. He is the source of goodness and the rule by which goodness is measured. A good God can do only good for those who love Him. See Psalm 25:8.

Holy God always exists in moral purity, and it is impossible for Him to be tainted by sin. He is so holy that no human can approach Him in his fallen state. This is what makes Christ's coming to earth so remarkable. See Exodus 3:5–6 and Revelation 4:8.

Immanent God is intimately involved in our lives, even the tiniest details of them. He orchestrates and uses all our moments for our good to bring Him glory. See Acts 17:27–28.

Immutable God does not change. His plans don't change. His character doesn't change. Nothing about Him changes. He is the same today as He was yesterday, and He will be the same tomorrow. See James 1:17.

Love God is more than loving; He is love. He is love in its truest embodiment, because He is the source of all true love. See Deuteronomy 7:7–8 and 1 John 4:8, 16.

Merciful God does not give us what we deserve—

punishment and death—but offers us His grace instead. See Romans 9:23–24 and Titus 3:5.

Omnipotent God has unlimited power to do whatever He wants. See Jeremiah 32:17 and Mark 14:36.

Omnipresent God is completely present in all places at all times. He is not constrained by time or space. He is fully Himself everywhere and always. See Psalm 139:7–10.

Omniscient God knows everything, for He is the source of all there is. No one can teach Him. He is never surprised. See Psalm 147:5 and Romans 11:33.

Self-existent God was not created and needs nothing from anyone or anything. See Exodus 3:14 and John 1:1–5.

Sovereign God has divine control over everything. He uses everything for our good and His glory. See Psalm 115:3 and Matthew 10:29.

Transcendent God's ways are higher and better than ours, and we will never be able to fully describe or understand Him. See Isaiah 55:8–9 and Psalm 113:5–6.

A Famine

Ruth 1:1–7

I LOVE TO EAT. I will tip up a bag of chips to get to those glorious flavor crystals that get stuck in the corners. I will polish off a dessert with my fork directly in the pan and not be ashamed. And don't even get me started on the rich aroma of a fresh cup of coffee. I enjoy a good meal with the best of them, and I am blessed to have never experienced the feeling of real, desperate hunger.

This was not so for the Israelites at the beginning of our study. It was the time "when the judges ruled" and "there was a famine in the land" (Ruth 1:1). With the opening lines we are thrust headfirst into a tragedy. The opening is meant to draw us in and take our breath away. But, spoiler alert, Ruth will end up being a breath of fresh air.

When the Judges Ruled

Read Ruth 1:1.

In setting up the story, the writer wants us to be aware of where we are. In the first verse we learn a lot about what faces the characters we will soon get to know.

1. When did the famine take place?

When the judges ruled

The judges were a group of individuals whom God strategically raised up to help wrangle in and rescue the rebellious Israelites. The judges were not casting judgment but were, rather, instruments to bring God's justice. The Israelites did not have a king other than the King of Kings, the Lord their God. They were meant to be self-ruling people who obeyed the laws and commands God had given them.

If you are familiar with the book of Judges, you will know that this period was not a pleasant time to be an Israelite. It immediately followed the death of Joshua, the one who had ushered the Chosen People into the Promised Land following the death of Moses. It had taken forty years of wandering before they were finally allowed to enter and make the place home. However, they couldn't just throw down a doormat and call it a day; they still had work to do.

2. According to the following passages, what were the people commanded to do / not to do?

Joshua 24:23 *Put away all the False gods or idols from among them*

Deuteronomy 20:17–18 *Destroy the people & drive them out*

The first command seems easy enough. They just needed to put away all the false gods, or idols, from among them. But those gods belonged to a powerful group or groups of people abiding in the land. The command in Deuteronomy tells us more about that.

The Israelites were told to destroy the people and drive them out. I don't know about you, but to me, at first glance this is shocking and seems downright cruel. Why would God give the command to completely destroy entire groups of people? On the surface it is absolutely confusing. But when we dive into the Scriptures, we find that this command is not given because of their race or the land. The people were so detestable, their ways so violent, and their sins so grievous that they simply could not be allowed to be that close to the Israelites in the land that God had promised them.

Their destruction was to be a direct result of their despicable sin. These were people who worshiped Chemosh and other false gods. But it wasn't like they just went to a different church than the Israelites. No, these people were steeped in a religion and culture that not only accepted but openly praised incest, adultery, child sacrifice, prostitution, sexual deviance, bestiality, and homosexuality. And they hated any and all who didn't accept or embrace their way of life. Imagine the Israelites moving in and pitching their tents or building their homes right in the midst of this open sin and idolatry and expecting to not be affected by it.

3. How did the Israelites do at driving out the people? For help, take a glance at Judges 1:27–33. *Not good. They failed to drive them out, they joined them*

Instead of driving out the inhabitants, the Israelites either moved in right next door or conquered them just enough to make them their slaves. So the customs and practices of the inhabitants, such as the Canaanites, remained and eventually corrupted the hearts of the Israelites, causing them to do just what Deuteronomy 20:18 warned would happen.

4. Read Psalm 81:8–13. According to this passage, what did God promise to do for the Israelites if they followed Him? *He would send a judge to deliver them*

5. But in verse 12 of Psalm 81, we read what they did instead. What was it? *They followed their own hearts lust + walked in their own counsel.*

During times of oppression or persecution, the Israelites would cry out to God, and God would send a judge to deliver them. But as soon as the judge died, the people would return to their old ways and repeat their mistakes over and over again.

They pursued other gods, and the Lord would give them over to their desires.

6. Have you ever desired something you shouldn't have, gotten it, and then realized it wasn't what you really wanted or needed?

7. Are there any enemies (sins, habits, relationships, etc.) that God has commanded you to conquer (drive out of your life) that you have refused to give up?

A Family in Crisis

Read Ruth 1:1–2 and Judges 6:1–6.

This is the world Elimelech and Naomi were trying to raise their children in. Nowhere was safe. Even the small town of Bethlehem wasn't off limits, and a famine was the result of living with the enemy. Because there is only one famine mentioned in the book of Judges, we are safe to assume that the one in Ruth and the one in Judges are one and the same; therefore, we will place Ruth's story here.

8. According to Judges 6:1–6, what was the cause of the famine? *The Israelites did all the labor of planting, etc., but were never allowed to enjoy the harvest*

9. Define *famine*.
A widespread shortage of food, water etc.

In the Western developed world, people don't know much of famine. We Americans have had glimpses of it in our history, and certainly we have suffered our share of catastrophes. When the Bible tells us there was a famine, particularly one affecting God's people, we ought to take notice.

The famines we know of are ones caused by lack of rain,

extreme heat, or other weather anomalies. But this one that threatened the lives of Elimelech and his family was of a different nature. The Israelites would be the ones sowing and reaping the food. They would watch the seeds turn to abundant crops; however, they would not get to taste of the harvest or have their bellies filled by it.

The Israelites became scavengers in the Promised Land, sneaking and hiding the food their own hands had gone to the dirt to grow. Elimelech and Naomi were right there, scared and scavenging. Another famine, in Genesis 12, drove Abram (later to be called Abraham) from Canaanite territory down to Egypt. There, in the process of fleeing the famine, Abram would make quite the blunder and almost lose his wife, Sarai, to Pharaoh (Genesis 12:10–20).

10. What do you think drove these two men (Abram and later Elimelech) to flee the famine?

In Genesis 12:10–20, Abram's decisions were driven by a desperation to save his wife and secure his future as the father of many nations (Genesis 17:6–8). To him, a famine posed a real threat to that promise. In the same way, it seems that Elimelech was a desperate man.

11. Have you ever been so desperate?

A Family of Faith

Read Ruth 1:2.

While Elimelech was desperate, he was also faithful. In the Bible, particularly in the Old Testament, a person's name was an indicator of his or her character. The name *Elimelech* means "My God is king." Coupled with *Naomi's* meaning of "pleasant" or "my delight" (and her faith we see in later passages), we get a picture of a family who loved and worshiped their Lord God. Elimelech was a faithful man who simply made a desperate move.

12. Naomi and Elimelech had two sons. What were their names? *Mahlon & Chilion*

The name *Mahlon* means "sickly," and *Chilion* means "wasting away" or "pining." The indication is clear: these boys were not healthy to begin with. Add to their condition a famine, which made food scarce, and you have the makings of a parental nightmare. When famine comes, it is only natural for people to run, so it is no surprise that we find this family leaving Bethlehem in search of relief.

13. Thoughtfully consider what you would do in Elimelech's or Naomi's situation. Would you begin to look for a place to go?

The Thing about Moab

The Moabites were descendants from Lot, Abraham's nephew, as a result of an incestuous relationship between Lot and his elder daughter (Genesis 19:30–38). The Moabites were worshipers of a particularly heinous idol, Chemosh. The rituals to the god Chemosh included temple prostitution, orgies, and human sacrifice (1 Kings 11:7; 2 Kings 3:26–27; Jeremiah 48). Lot and his family had been strongly influenced by the sex- and violence-obsessed culture of Sodom and Gomorrah while they lived there, and they carried it with them to Moab (Genesis 19:1–11).

Tension and often hatred existed between the Israelites and the Moabites (Judges 3:12–30). Obviously, Moab was a place that no self-respecting Israelite would go. Therefore, for a Jehovah-fearing man like Elimelech to take his family there, he must have been experiencing a great deal of suffering in Israel and saw no hope of immediate relief.

While we can make lots of healthy speculations, I am not sure we can really know if Elimelech's move to Moab was good or bad. In fact, I'm not sure it really matters for our purposes. What we do know is that He was a loving father and tried to be a faithful Israelite. But he was faced with desperate circumstances. And so the family left relatives, friends, and home in Bethlehem and settled in Moab. Our story reveals that, unfortunately, over the course of ten years, Elimelech died, his sons married two Moabite women, and then his sons also died.

The Gospel

Faith and Trust

Personally, I've never felt the lingering ache of real hunger, the debilitating emptiness of starvation, or even the threat of such an existence. I can't relate to the fear that must have engulfed Elimelech when he thought of the safety of his precious family.

However, I do know the lingering ache of uncertainty and the debilitating emptiness of fear. I know well the threat of financial loss or, worse, the scent of disease and the death it inevitably brings. I know the desperation that leads us to turn over every stone and search every corner for an answer or an escape. I also know what it's like to look to God as the last resort instead of the first person we turn to in answering these woes.

Our spiritual famine, lack, and weaknesses naturally make us want to run, seek greener grass, and shore ourselves up. But the great news is that when we are presented with a famine, God doesn't abandon us.

14. In your own words, define *faith*.

15. In your own words, define *trust*.

16. What do you think the main difference is between faith and
    trust?

It seems that Elimelech had faith in the Lord, but perhaps he
lacked trust. I can relate. Can you? For example, I find it easy to
have faith that Jesus has redeemed me and that I face the joyful
promise of eternity with Him. But, in contrast, I find it most difficult to trust God for the everyday trials. Will I see Him face-to-
face in Heaven one day? Absolutely! Will He provide for my daily
strength right now? Unfortunately, I am sometimes debilitated
by doubt.

It's in these everyday, common, ordinary moments that it is
most easy to lose sight of God. We forget that He is a God Who
delights in the details. In fact, the entire book of Ruth shows us
a God Who delights in orchestrating the details. We call it God's
immanence.

He is not a God Who sits high on His throne completely and
totally removed from the creation He spoke into being. He is
intimately involved in every moment, everywhere, all the time.
Nothing escapes His notice. And His providence tells us that
He uses all of these moments for our good. Yes, God can even
use our mistakes, fears, and faithlessness to compose a story we
wouldn't dream could ever be our own.

The Real Need

So, at the end of Ruth 1:5, we find three women suddenly
forced into a situation they never would have wanted. In a culture and time when widows were often neglected and left desti-
tute, the situation couldn't have been much worse.

17. Reflect over the verses we've seen in Judges 1, 3, and 6. What was the root of all this devastation?

We see in Ruth 1:1 a good family suffering because of the sins of others. Our sins don't affect just us. Our sins can affect our families and communities, both in the moment and for generations to come. The Bible tells us that by one man, sin entered the world (Romans 5:12). While we have sinned enough on our own to warrant condemnation and death, it was by Adam's sin that every life after him and all of the world has been marred by the effects of sin: death, disease, illness, tragedy, catastrophe, hatred, racism, war, lying, gossip, betrayal, famine, and eternal separation from God.

18. Why do we like to think our sins don't affect other people?

Our sins are not little secrets that we keep high on a shelf perfectly hidden from human eyes. They are cancerous tumors that, when left, grow and devour and kill. However, the effects of our sin, unlike cancer, are contagious. Sin spreads, casting its shadow far and wide.

19. How have you seen your sin or the sins of another tragically affect a community, family, or generations?

The famine that touched the Israelites is a perfect example of sin's destruction. We can see that not all the Israelites had their hearts turned from following Jehovah. But there were enough to warrant a reckoning with God that everyone, including Elimelech and Naomi, had to face.

Weakness, loss, grief, and famine are the perfect setting for a rescue. God didn't miss the intimate details of this family's lives—the everyday decisions that perhaps seemed so meaningless and ordinary. Nothing escaped His attention. He saw it all, and He was planning to use it all.

Tragedy and grief define the first seven verses of Ruth. A nation was being gutted as a result of their own sin. A family sought relief but found death. Three wives lost their husbands. One wife also lost her sons. But the bloodline of the Promised One was pulsing in our story, even through desperation, empty hands, and brokenness.

God can do a lot with someone who has empty hands. It's at the end of our own efforts and striving that the gospel first gets ahold of our hearts. Oftentimes we must be emptied to be filled back up. Our brokenness drives us to reach out and grab hold of Jesus' nail-pierced hands. And, because of this, we can be thankful for our desperate and broken parts. But, praise God, this is only the beginning of the story.

Personal Application

What does this tell me about God?

Which of God's attributes is displayed in Ruth 1:1–7?

How can I apply this to my life?

A Friendship

Ruth 1:6–18

HOW HEARTBREAKING to see that the people of God had fallen so far from their Lord that Bethlehem, which means the "House of Bread," had to be stripped of its bread. But how glorious these words from Ruth 1:6 are: "The LORD had visited His people." He had not left them. He had not forgotten them. He had not abandoned them. He eagerly awaited their return to Him, and when He heard their cries, Jehovah gladly gave the House of Bread the bread it was lacking.

Ten More Years

1. Write out the verse which reveals that Jehovah gladly gave the House of Bread the bread it was lacking.

2. The famine in Judges lasted seven years (Judges 6:1). From our reading in lesson 1, do you remember how long Naomi was in Moab?

It could be that Naomi and her sons had heard that the famine had ended but that the boys had their eyes on two Moabite women and decided to stay. Perhaps the sons had already died and Naomi lingered with her daughters-in-law. For whatever reason, Naomi was still in Moab after ten years. The situation for a woman without a husband, particularly in a pagan society like Moab, was dire. Once she heard that the famine had ended and the "LORD had visited His people," Naomi certainly spent time considering her options: stay or return.

In Bethlehem she would have Elimelech's land, which she would be incapable of tending, but at least that would lend the possibility of an income if she sold it. Although the future wasn't promising in either location, Naomi decided Bethlehem was where she needed to be. After all, if nothing else, it was home.

3. What things might have prompted Naomi to stay in Moab instead of return to Bethlehem?

A Convincing Argument

The three women began the journey to Bethlehem together, but it doesn't look like they made it far. Perhaps as they walked, Naomi played thoughts over in her mind, and doubts surfaced, causing her to plead with her daughters-in-law to return to their homes instead of traveling any farther with her.

Naomi wasn't urging them to leave her because she didn't love them; it was her love for them that prompted her change of heart.

4. In what ways do we see Naomi's love for her daughters-in-law (and them for her) in Ruth 1:7–14?

Naomi loved her daughters-in-law so much that she felt it was truly best for them both to return to their own families.

A woman of her age and situation had no way of providing for herself, much less for two others. In addition, Ruth and Orpah would be taking great risk to go with Naomi to a place where they would be foreigners and outcasts.

Naomi used some well-reasoned arguments to convince Ruth and Orpah to leave. They were effective enough to convince Orpah, but Ruth was different. She withstood three arguments from Naomi that each challenged her in relation to three natural desires.

Let's look at them.

Argument 1

Read Ruth 1:8–9.

5. What desire of Ruth's did this argument appeal to?

The first argument appeals to Ruth's desire for home, two homes in fact. One house would provide immediate relief. The second house would provide hope for the future.

6. Which two "houses" did Naomi mention in verses 8 and 9?

There is nothing like a mother's touch when it comes to either a scraped-up knee or a banged-up heart. And a home with a husband would appeal to a woman's natural desire for a family of her very own. Surprisingly, this argument didn't work on either of the young women. Verses 9 and 14 of chapter 1 are so vivid in their description of the anguish of leaving each other that it is clear the girls had an obvious bond with their mother-in-law. This bond was just as strong, if not stronger, than the one they had with their own mothers.

Argument 2

Read Ruth 1:11–13.

7. What desire of Ruth's did this argument appeal to?

While the desire for home is natural, the desire for a secure future is much more compelling, especially considering what Naomi was laying in front of them. By telling Ruth and Orpah that she had no more sons in her womb, she was reminding them that there was no hope for marriage if they continued with her. Marriage meant a husband; a husband meant security. The only thing that faced them in Bethlehem was perpetual widowhood and poverty.

8. In verse 13, what grieves Naomi?

Naomi loved her daughters-in-law and feared for their future. But simply by turning back to Moab and to their homes, they would easily remarry, have children, and create a secure future—this devastation could soon be a vague memory and nothing more. This was enough for Orpah; she said her goodbyes and left Naomi and Ruth.

Argument 3

Read Ruth 1:15.

9. What desire of Ruth's did this argument appeal to?

The third argument was Naomi's final attempt. Surely now that Orpah had turned toward home, Ruth would be more easily compelled to follow. So Naomi pleaded with Ruth's desire for comfort—the comfort of familiar people, familiar practices, and familiar gods. Ruth could easily step back into her previous life and return to all the comforts she had known before.

10. What three things did Naomi list as part of Ruth's "comfort zone" in verse 15?

No doubt, part of Ruth longed for the familiar comfort zone that didn't require any amount of sacrifice. Following Orpah would usher her back to comfort, security, and home. In contrast, following Naomi would remove all comfort she had ever known—there would be no familiar streets, familiar faces (save for Naomi's), familiar smells, or familiar voices. But Ruth was a woman who eschewed the comforts of familiarity in favor of something so much more.

11. If you had been called to make a big change or take a giant step of faith, what three things could someone use to convince you to abandon the mission?

A Convincing Response

Ruth's response to Naomi's arguments is one of the most beautiful statements of commitment and faith in all the Scriptures. It is so poetic, selfless, and filled with such tender expressions of love that it has become a part of many marriage ceremonies; however, it is not a commitment of marital love or affection. It is a deep commitment of loyal friendship.

12. Copy Ruth's statement (below) and consider memorizing it. (There is extra space on page 32.)

Entreat me not to leave you,
Or to turn back from following after you;
For wherever you go, I will go;
And wherever you lodge, I will lodge;
Your people shall be my people,
And your God, my God.
Where you die, I will die,
And there will I be buried.
The LORD do so to me, and more also,
If anything but death parts you and me.

Response 1

Not only did Ruth shut down Naomi's arguments with loyal determination, but she also answered each of her arguments directly. For example, Naomi's first argument targeted Ruth's desire for home and a relationship born out of a lifelong motherly connection. However, Ruth responded by committing herself bodily as if to say, "You are my family now." When Ruth said, "Wherever you lodge, I will lodge," she was telling Naomi that a home with her was the home she needed. Ruth would stick so close as to require the same house, no matter how meager the quarters.

Response 2

Naomi's second argument appealed to Ruth's desire for security, a very real need for a young widow. But Ruth retorted, "Wherever you go, I will go." Ruth was promising to share in all the physical and financial burden that Naomi carried. And, because of Naomi's great age, Ruth knew that by doing so she was taking on most of the burden alone. By following Naomi to Bethlehem, she was committing to walk in Naomi's footsteps, follow her lead, and learn from her like a daughter from a mother, despite the risky circumstances it would place her in.

Response 3

Naomi's third argument was aimed at Ruth's desire for the familiarity of her comfort zone. When Ruth said, "Your people shall by my people," she was saying that she was forsaking everything she knew—all the people of her past, all the tradition, and their land—to become like an Israelite.

Typically when people immigrate to the United States from a foreign country, they bring a lot of their traditions with them: food, music, culture, and religion. They become Americans but also maintain a sense of who they are based on their history and their natural ethnicity.

13. What do you think Ruth was saying when she said, "Your people shall be my people"?

Ruth was not only declaring that she was making the move to become a citizen of Israel. Her statement is so declarative as to say they were her "people." She was making the Israelite nation both her future and her past. She was promising to cast off all tradition and culture, as if it never was, in order to fully embrace the people of Israel as her own.

And then she declared that the God of Naomi would be her God. This is huge, particularly considering what Ruth had witnessed in Naomi's life.

Who in her right mind would want to be an Israelite right then? Sure, the famine had ended, but Ruth had seen firsthand what life for an Israelite was like. Based on what she had witnessed in the lives of her in-laws, and surely what she had heard of Israelites' recent history as a nation, she knew that the road would be hard, the people would be different, and the enemies were abundant.

Her in-laws had fled their home because they were Israelites. They had suffered greatly because they were Israelites. The Israelites as a whole were rebellious and fickle. Yet there Ruth was, declaring not only that she wanted to be an Israelite but that she wanted to follow their God.

A Friendship That Changed a Life

It can be said that Ruth easily countered all three of Naomi's arguments with this statement of commitment to both Naomi and her God. But it doesn't sound like this was an epiphany for Ruth. Naomi's questioning was just a window of opportunity for

Ruth to share her faith and throw both arms fully around what had already begun to take root in her heart in the past.

14. Why do you think Ruth was so drawn to Jehovah, the God of the Israelites?

Many people read the life and words of Naomi and they picture a woman of little, or at least waning, faith. However, if Naomi had been as faithless as we are often led to believe, the Lord would have been even less appealing to Ruth. It is more likely, however, that Ruth's strong faith was the result of Naomi's faithful testimony—both in word and action—of the power, compassion, and redemptive plan of Jehovah.

15. Would your words, actions, and attitudes be a powerful testimony for Christ or would they be a testimony against Christ?

16. In what ways can our lives be a testimony for Christ?

17. In the reverse, in what ways can our lives be a testimony against Christ?

The Final Word

As if Ruth's answers to Naomi's arguments hadn't been enough, Ruth ended with a statement that can easily make us Americans say, Huh?: "The LORD do so to me, and more also, if anything but death parts you and me."

There you have it. No room for doubt. No room for additional questions. The argument was nailed shut with this sentence. This was not a run-of-the-mill closing argument; this was a promise made in the name of the Lord to solidify Ruth's commitment and remove any doubt from Naomi's mind. Essentially Ruth's words mean "God is my witness that death, death, and only death will be able to separate me from you."

The Gospel

Ruth was dedicated to her mother-in-law and wanted to remain a part of her family. She was also dedicated to Jehovah and wanted to be a part of His people. Her words were strong and her decision was set; there was no reason for further discussion.

18. What shared characteristic of Ruth and Naomi do we see in Ruth 1:18?

We have two determined women grasping hands and linking arms with their faces set toward Bethlehem. Many generations later this place would again be visited by God, but this time more than just bread would be given. The Bread of Life, the Messiah Himself, would be born (Matthew 2:1).

From the moment of Adam and Eve's sin, a Redeemer was promised, One Who would crush the serpent's head and make right the people's sins. The Lord promised Abraham in Genesis 22:18 that in his seed "all the nations of the earth shall be blessed." Even before the Messiah was revealed in human flesh, died, and rose again, the promise of His coming was engraved on the hearts of true believers from Genesis onward.

By all accounts, Ruth should not have anticipated that Jehovah would want her. She was a young woman raised in a pagan culture, she was not of the right ethnicity, and she didn't have the right creed, upbringing, or education. She was a Gentile—not one of God's Chosen People. Yet by God's grace upon her, she understood that salvation through faith is available to all, not just the Jews.

Ruth believed in the coming Messiah, and she believed in the promise that the Messiah would be one for "all nations." But Ruth's belief didn't come without sacrifice. This is what we love to forget in our modern and abundant society. Yes, belief in Jesus Christ as our Lord and Savior is a blessing beyond description, but it is also a sacrificial belief. We are called to lay everything down. It is only by losing our life that we are able to find it (Matthew 10:39).

19. Read Matthew 10:39. In what ways have you had to lose your life to Christ? Or what ways do you think that God may be calling you to lose your life?

The gospel is counterintuitive; it flies in the face of our natural desires for self-glorification and self-preservation. When our hands are emptied, as we discussed in lesson 1, we expect to have them filled back up with health, wealth, and prosperity. But the good news of the gospel is not that our hands will be filled; it is that our hope will be found, that a relationship with God will be restored, and that our eternity will be secure to the glory of God, not to the glory of self.

When Ruth made her poetic commitment to Naomi and to the Lord she was not committing herself to a friend or a God Who would always make her happy by giving her the best of everything on earth. Instead she was making a commitment to the Lord, Who, despite all the weariness of the world, could sustain her with hope, joy, and peace. She had been drawn to what so many of us for years and years to come will be drawn to—the wooing of a God Who loves us and gave Himself for us (Ephesians 5:2).

Ruth told Naomi that only death would separate them. The good news for believers is that death can't separate us from God. In fact, it brings us face-to-face with Him. But this is only if we have confessed our need for a Savior and embraced the truth of the gospel. The bad news is that we are sinners bound for an eternal punishment in Hell. The Good News (the gospel) is that God's love for us moved Him to send His Son, Jesus Christ, to take the punishment for our sins so we may be redeemed from Hell and cast into the light of His glorious grace. This gives us eternal life in Heaven in the presence of God, and hope for a life that can bring glory to God here on this earth.

Imagine that! The life we live here on earth has the potential to bring glory to God. When we suffer, we can bring God glory. When we prosper, we can bring God glory. In the valleys, we can bring God glory. On the mountaintops, we can bring God glory. And everywhere in between, through the power of the Holy Spirit working within us, we can bring God glory.

Jesus, Friend of Sinners

Ruth had a friend in Naomi and Naomi a friend in Ruth. But the friendship that really bound them was the one with the promised Messiah. We are the blessed ones! Ruth and Naomi hoped for a Messiah to come, but we can trust in a Messiah that has already come and lives within those who believe! If you find yourself envying the friendship between Ruth and Naomi, remember that the best friend you can have is Christ.

He is the friend of sinners, but not in that He disregards, condones, brushes off, or justifies the sin. He is a friend of sinners in such a way that He came to save sinners and it is His pleasure to do so. While we were still sinners, He died for us (Romans 5:8). And there is no greater love to be had than from the one who lays down his life for friends (John 15:13). Jesus loves embracing repentant sinners and covering them with His blood.

Personal Application

What does this tell me about God?

Which of God's characteristics is displayed in Ruth 1:6–18?

How can I apply this to my life?

A Faith

Ruth 1:16–22

FAITH: WE SAY WE HAVE IT, we attach blessings to it, and we pray for it. We have it in the airplane pilot who takes us from point A to point B. We have it in politicians when we select their names on our ballots. And, as children, we have it in our parents as we leap free from the ledge, trusting their arms to catch us.

Hebrews 11:1 defines faith as "the substance of things hoped for, the evidence of things not seen." The passage continues from there, commending Old Testament people for their faith, using the term "by faith." With that in mind, we can say that "by faith" Ruth followed Naomi into Bethlehem. Ruth was a great example of what saving faith in the Lord looks like. But Ruth isn't the only one we can look at to see such faith displayed. In the passages that follow Ruth's beautiful words, we see a different kind of proclamation of faith, one that had found itself weighted by grief.

A Grieving Faith

Read Ruth 1:19–22.

In our reading we see that as Naomi and Ruth arrived in Bethlehem, their presence caused quite a stir. Word spread quickly, and the town center was turned into what seemed like a buzzing hive of activity. In fact, we get the impression that the townspeople were fluttering about with the news.

I've heard it said that it isn't easy to go home. In Naomi's case this was certainly true. As women came out to greet Naomi, they called her by name and delighted in seeing their old friend home again. Naomi, however, stamped out their thrill with a heartbreaking lament.

1. Write out Naomi's words from Ruth 1:20–21.

2. Now, rewrite them using your own words. Try to capture the pain and grief. Consider using some of your own past or current grief to articulate what Naomi was communicating.

3. The meaning of Mara is the opposite of "pleasant." What does the name Mara mean?

Naomi's Lament

In Naomi we see a woman who was unable to connect with the person she had once been, due to the bitter hand she had been given. So she asked to be called "bitter." Although her display of loss and grief was jarring, particularly compared to Ruth's display of faith, Naomi's words are something many of us can relate to. And if we can't now, there may likely be a time when we will.

In fact, another in the Bible has a very close connection to Naomi by a similar expression of grief. Consider the word that

Naomi used for God in verses 20 and 21. She called Him "the LORD" twice and "the Almighty" twice.

"The LORD" was the official, proper name of the One True God, or Jehovah (YHWH in Hebrew). "The Almighty" is the translation of the word *Shadday,* which is used forty-eight times in the Bible. Thirty of those occasions are found in one book alone.

4. Which Old Testament book uses the word *Shadday* thirty times? Hint: the words were spoken by a man known for his immense suffering.

If there was one person in the Bible, probably in all of history, who understood grief and loss better than anyone else, it would be Job. Job lost everything: his children, his home, his health, his property, and all his possessions. Interestingly, it seems the only people who were spared were his three friends and his wife—none of whom were much help (Job 2:9; 42:7–9).

Job's words, recorded for us in the book that bears his name, are poignant and painfully real. But, looking at them side by side, you can see the similarities between the grief both Job and Naomi expressed.

Job (Job 1:21)	Naomi (Ruth 1:21; 2:20)
"Naked I came from my mother's womb, and naked shall I return there. The LORD gave, and the LORD has taken away; blessed be the name of the LORD."	"I went out full, and the LORD has brought me home again empty. Why do you call me Naomi, since the LORD has testified against me, and the Almighty has afflicted me? . . . Blessed be he of the LORD, who has not forsaken His kindness to the living and the dead!"

Their words share more similarities in context and stylistic expression; they share in acknowledging Who God is and what He does.

Faith in the Lord, Yahweh

The word translated "the LORD" was the personal name of God in Hebrew. You may see it as YHWH, or Jehovah, as well. However you see it spelled or translated, the meaning is the same.

5. When God introduced Himself to Moses in Exodus 3:14, whom did God say He was?

This was the name God gave Himself and is the most all-encompassing descriptor of His character and existence. When His people called Him the Lord, Yahweh, or Jehovah, it was an acknowledgement of His "I AM" status.

"I AM" means God is all-existent with no beginning and no end. It means He is all-sufficient; He needs nothing from any-one. He is absolutely independent. He is constant and unchanging. He doesn't need permission. He does what He wants, and what He does is always right. He is everything to everyone, what every person needs.

6. In light of this, what do you think Naomi was saying when she called God "Yahweh"?

Faith in the Almighty, Shadday

Both Job and Naomi had a way with words, particularly when they used the word *Shadday* to express God's sovereignty in their lives; this sovereignty included His control over their loss.

The obvious implication of the word *Shadday* is for the strength of the Lord, since we see the word translated "the Al-mighty." A slight variance on the name is El-Shaddai, which was one of the ancient names known for God before He fully revealed Himself to the people as Yahweh.

Genesis 17:1 says, "When Abram was ninety-nine years old, the LORD appeared to Abram and said to him, 'I am Almighty God; walk before Me and be blameless.'" To call Him the Almighty was to acknowledge His omnipotence. The word *omnipotence* is defined as "having all power." Job and Naomi both understood that God has all power, in all circumstances, in all places, in all ways.

Faith in His Sovereignty

These two names, Shadday and Yahweh, point us toward Naomi's ability to see God's sovereignty. If God is all things and has all power, then He is sovereign.

7. Write out your understanding of the word *sovereign*.

The sovereignty of God is the combination of His strength and His power; it is His ultimate authority. His authority over us comes from the fact that He created us and everything else, for that matter. Psalm 100:3 puts it this way: "Know that the LORD, He is God; it is He who has made us, and not we ourselves; we are His people and the sheep of His pasture."

Remember when we talked about the differences between faith and trust? This is right where this hits us between the eyes. The cause of our inability to trust is in our inability to fully understand God's sovereignty in our lives, both in the good and in what we would call the bad.

It was hard for me to look into the eyes of my friend following her miscarriage and not feel some questioning of why God allows what He allows. It is hard for me to listen to the ache of another woman whose husband has been dramatically changed by a terminal disease and not wonder what our sovereign God could possibly be thinking.

God's sovereignty does not mean all is well all the time. It means that all things that happen are for our good (Romans 8:28). Our definition of *good* is flawed, because what God sees as good often looks painful to our human eyes. But our good is always to bring Him glory. And since goodness is in His very nature, our good God can do only good.

Naomi understood in the same way Job did that the Lord gives and the Lord takes away. I urge you to read Naomi's words not as a complaint against God but instead as a theological grasp of God's very nature. Was she happy about what had happened? No! But she knew that His hand was in her sufferings, just as it had been in her blessings.

While her words hang with a bitter fragrance, they are not bitterness of heart. Naomi had been given a bitter pill to swallow. Anyone, even the most saintly, who experiences the loss that Naomi did would certainly cry out with similar words of pain. But her words are not blaming God; her words are simply giving attention to the sovereign God, Who knows all things, and the Almighty God, Whose will was better than her own.

The Gospel

We have seen Naomi's faith in God's sovereignty. Now we will look deeper at Ruth's faith in God's salvation. In last week's lesson we reviewed Ruth's commitment to Naomi in detail. Now we will go back to review the same statement in light of how it reflects our commitment to God as believers. Let's slowly taste the richness of her words and the truth contained.

Wherever You Go, I Will Go

The gospel is grace given to us. We do not earn it; we do not buy it; we do not deserve it. In fact, we would not even seek it were it not for the moving of the Holy Spirit first prompting us. We are the sheep following His leading and responding to His calling. Like Ruth, our first step in faith is to say, "Yes, wherever You go, I will go."

Wherever You Lodge, I Will Lodge

Once the step is taken, we are called to abide in Him. This is not an actual shared residence, as Ruth was promising to Naomi, but a full and total surrender to making ourselves wholly and completely His. We abide in Him like fruit abides in a vine (John 15:4). Without the vine, the fruit dies. The Lord God is our dwelling place. In Him we live, move, and have our being (Acts 17:28).

Your People Shall Be My People

The Christian life is not meant to be lived in autonomy. We live in a strange culture where people exist with a real fear of missing out, but also cling tightly to their sense of individualism.

I have watched many people get upset when they weren't invited to an event, only to say no when they were later invited. I have even heard them say, "I just wanted to be invited, even though I didn't really want to go."

Of course it's great to be invited, and that's exactly what Christ did and what, therefore, His church should be doing. However, the problem isn't usually the lack of an invite; the real problem is in our lack of understanding how much we actually need each other.

It's the buddy system of the Christian life, and that's not limited to attending church services, although it's definitely included. This is the buddy system that meets for coffee, picks up the phone to ask for prayer when crises hit, comes over in the middle of the night when a friend's child is sick, brings dinner, calls just because, and gets together for no good reason. This is also the buddy system that challenges, exhorts, encourages, and speaks the truth with love. All of this is a part of being a member of the church, with the most imperative being the regular gathering of the local church body.

Those who neglect the church buddy system often fall in one of three categories. One, they see gathering as important but fail to connect on any level other than cursory and superficial. Two, they gather here and there, serial dating lots of churches and lots of groups without any commitment. Three, they see church as useless and outdated. These are usually the people we hear saying, "I love Jesus, but I don't love the church [or Christians]." What they don't know is that you can't love Jesus and not love Christians (1 John 2:3–23). To love Jesus is to love your fellow believers.

Your God, My God

God requires lordship of our lives. God doesn't just want our eternity; He requires our present. Often we dethrone God in our hearts by seeking our way, our will, our desires, and our comfort. But an eternity given to God means a life surrendered to God now. He will accept nothing less.

When I sit on the throne of my heart, I am dysfunctional at best. It takes a daily—and sometimes moment-by-moment—discipline to submit to Him. We can dethrone the Lord without even realizing it as we get comfortable and complacent. But He is still Lord of our right here and right now. I find the best way to remember this is to regularly ask the Lord to remind me of His presence today. Sometimes I miss it still. But many times, through nature, my children, music, and the regular rhythms of life, He whispers, and I am reminded of His nearness. When I am reminded of His nearness, I have another opportunity to step away from the throne of my heart and bow to the rightful sovereign.

Where You Die, I Will Die

Yes, our faith has eternal consequences. This life is not just here and now. The gospel makes an extraordinary promise of extraordinary grace to us who believe: when we close our eyes on earth in death, we will see Jesus face-to-face. However, the promise of eternal punishment is just as real for those who have not acknowledged Christ as the Lord Whom they need to save them from their sins. If you find yourself in this first group, you have many reasons to praise God today. If you find yourself in the latter group, you have many reasons to repent to God today.

Saving Faith Leads to Action

Saving faith leads to action. Ruth didn't sit on her hands, wearing her faith as a crutch. Instead her faith led her to see the Lord's provision right in front of her in the ability to glean. And then she put in the effort required. There is a time to be still, but there is also a time to act. Our saving faith often calls us to action—the action of service, of giving, of time, of ministry, of putting our hands to the work that God has called us to.

Two Women; One Faith

We see Ruth displaying beautiful faith that is full of hope. We see Naomi displaying beautiful faith that is full of wisdom. One is fresh and new. The other is wise from a life already lived. While Ruth's faith-filled words on the road to Bethlehem are beautiful, Naomi's faith-filled lament is powerful and honest.

Through Naomi's and Ruth's eyes and in their words, we get to see a multifaceted faith that encompasses joy and sorrow, opportunity and defeat, highs and lows. We see two very different women with a shared faith in an almighty, sovereign God, Who through every circumstance works for their good and for His glory.

Personal Application

What does this tell you about God?

Which of God's character traits do you see showcased in Ruth 1:16—2:7?

How can you apply this to your life?

A Foreigner

Ruth 2:1–23

AS THE SUN BEGAN TO CAST ITS RAYS over the horizon, I imagine Ruth was taking her first steps onto the soil. As she moved solemnly and steadily through the field, the golden heads of grain brushed her cheeks and crunched under her feet. The sun rose higher as she continued to pick her way behind the reapers, one row after another. They noticed her; she was different.

A man named Boaz owned the field. When he arrived, he, too, noticed the girl. Something about her presence, her dress, her way of moving, or her voice would have marked her as a foreigner. The owner asked the lead reaper who the girl was. Perhaps the answer confirmed what Boaz already suspected.

Yes, he had heard of her. Stories like hers spread quickly, and it was an impressive one. He welcomed her with praise for her love and loyalty to her mother-in-law, gave her a quick lesson on gleaning etiquette, invited her to eat with the reapers, and then finally made sure she would be well provided for and protected while in his field.

At the end of a long day, Ruth was able to return to Naomi with a load of barley. It was impressive, to say the least. Imagine that. Ruth, an ordinary foreigner, finding such favor with a man like Boaz.

I Am a Foreigner

Read Ruth 2:10–14.

While Ruth had surrendered the life she had known before and had embraced a new life with new people and their God, she still couldn't shake the feeling of being not like them. Twice during their conversation, Ruth told Boaz that she was a foreigner and not like his maidservants. This wasn't news to Boaz; he was well acquainted with her story.

But Ruth still couldn't fathom why an upstanding and faithful man like Boaz was showing her so much grace. He didn't care she wasn't an Israelite; she was the one who seemed to be bothered by it.

But she wasn't the first ordinary person, foreigner, or outcast to come to the Lord. This is a common theme in many Biblical accounts of God or Christ interacting with someone who was of foreign blood.

1. Look up the following passages and note where the foreigner was from and what God or Christ did for him or her.
   Genesis 16:1, 7–10, 13

   Luke 17:12–19

   Joshua 2; 6:25

An Egyptian slave, a Samaritan leper, and a Canaanite prostitute were not just foreigners; some would have even been outcasts in their own societies. God blessed them, rescued them, and redeemed them. As a Gentile myself, I'm excited by these passages. I rejoice knowing that from the very beginning of time and creation, God planned to redeem me and that His promises to do so are sprinkled heavily in His Word.

In the field, Boaz spoke kindly to Ruth, praising her for her faithful commitment. He then encouraged her to stay in his field and continue to glean without fear of being hurt or driven away. For Ruth, Boaz's kind words and blessings to her in the field would have been enough, but Boaz knew something that Ruth had yet to fully comprehend: God doesn't just tolerate foreigners; He loves them!

2. Ruth 2:14 recounts a remarkable move that is reminiscent of Christ at the well with the Samaritan woman. What did Boaz do?

Ruth didn't sit and eat alone, but "she sat beside the reapers" and ate of their shared bread (Ruth 2:14). In Boaz's eyes she was one of them. She just needed to fully accept it too.

The Moabite Woman and the Canaanite Prostitute

The town had been abuzz with excitement when Naomi returned home empty-handed, save for this girl. No doubt about it, the girl was different. While any physical differences may have been slight, perhaps the way she held a gaze or the way she tied a dress would have been indicators that she wasn't an Israelite. Despite her foreign status and outsider ways, Ruth, in her short time in Bethlehem, had already made a name for herself.

3. Next to each passage, write the character trait you see displayed.
   Ruth 1:14

   Ruth 1:16–17

Ruth 1:18

Ruth 2:2

Ruth 2:7

Ruth 2:10

Ruth 2:17

Ruth 2:18

Ruth 2:23

Ruth was hardworking, faithful, humble, determined, grateful, kind, and full of hope. In the brief time she was in Bethlehem, these traits had already been seen and duly noted. Needless to say, she was making an impression.

The people had just come out of a long time of oppression at the hands of the foreigners around them; they would have been right to be a tad bit suspicious of this Moabite's presence among them. Their suffering had been great, and their defenses would be high. But Boaz showed true compassion and concern for Ruth. Strange, yes, until you learn of the other foreign woman, Rahab, whom Boaz was well acquainted with.

4. According to Matthew 1:5, how did Boaz know Rahab?

Rahab was a Canaanite living high on the wall surrounding Jericho. The location on the wall provided her ample opportunity to peddle her business as a prostitute. In addition, she may have even been a prominent rich woman in her community, since the Canaanites didn't despise prostitution, like they should have. The Israelite spies were clever in going to her place to hide, since they would get entry to her home easily and with little questioning from the woman of the house.

For her part, Rahab would be accustomed to hiding men and keeping secrets. However, what the spies didn't expect was her response. Israel was a mighty nation whose reputation had preceded them. Rahab told them that the people had great fear in their hearts because they had heard how the Lord had delivered the Jews from the Egyptians. Surely "He is God in heaven above and on earth beneath," she said (Joshua 2:11). In her way, she was telling them that *she* believed in the Lord God Almighty. Because of her actions and her faith, she was able to save not only herself from the Israelite invasion but also her family.

    5. According to Joshua 6:25, what did Rahab do after the invasion and the dust had settled?

Much like Ruth, Rahab had chosen a new people, abandoned everything she had known, and embraced the Lord God of the Israelites as her own. Perhaps when Boaz looked at Ruth, he remembered his mother and the stories she had told, the way she had comforted him, and the things she had taught him. He knew, firsthand, the beauty of a foreign woman coming to the Israelites and to their God.

It is one thing to speak faithful commitment with your lips, but it is something entirely different when it actually changes you. Ruth and Rahab had both been changed as their faith permeated their words, beliefs, and actions, causing them to abandon everything they knew to follow the Lord.

An Ephah of Barley

Read Ruth 2:15–18.

Boaz was aware of the struggles Ruth would face as a foreign widow. And, much like his mother Rahab, Ruth had a family to take care of. Naomi was too old to glean, and Ruth had electively taken on the role of provider. Even the men who reaped ahead of Ruth recognized her value, as one of them noted that she "has continued from morning until now, though she rested a little" (Ruth 2:7).

6. Boaz gave special instructions to the reapers in his field. What were they?

Because of the clear instruction Boaz gave his men, Ruth returned home to Naomi with an ephah of barley. An ephah is an ancient measurement. In the US imperial system of measurement this would be about forty pounds. Did you read that? Forty pounds of barley! That was enough to feed both Ruth and Naomi for weeks.

Ruth had only been a watchful eye when the Israelites suffered famine at the hands of the Canaanites. Her shared suffering wasn't in an empty belly but in an empty home. However, she did share with them in their obedience. In lesson 1 we noted that disobedience doesn't hurt just us but has a ripple effect on others. The same can be said for obedience! As Ruth walked home with forty pounds of barley, she carried with her the result of the Chosen People turning their hearts back to God. She was a beneficiary of the relationship God had with His people.

The Gospel

We, too, can be beneficiaries of such a relationship. Because of Christ, we are now offered a place at the table; we can now be a part of the reapers; we are able to grasp hold of the full reward from the Lord God of Israel. The death of Jesus Christ, God's only Son, was the fulfillment of the promise to Adam and Eve, Abraham and Sarah, and Jacob (Genesis 3:15; 22:18; 28:14). Jesus Christ was the promise that would bless all nations, not just the nation of Israel. And that blessing is the promise of eternal life and relationship with God.

Have you ever been an outsider? Have you ever walked into a room and looked around to find that you don't belong? I think probably everyone has at some point. And for that, we are in good company.

Christ, too, was an outsider. He came in an unexpected way as a poor baby in obscure standing. While raised as a devout Israelite, He still stuck out like a sore thumb. The Bible says that He amazed the crowds because He spoke as an authority and not like the leaders (Matthew 7:28–29). He didn't court the Pharisees and, instead, ate with sinners, made disciples out of ordinary people, and healed the sick with power they couldn't comprehend. He went from being adored one moment to being hated the next.

And because Christ was an outsider, we, too, are outsiders. Those who believe in Christ are strangers in this world (John 15:18–19; Philippians 3:20). Our treasure is not here on earth, and our eyes are fixed on a future home. That home is free of sin, guilt, shame, disease, death, and hate. This world will cause us to ache; it will make us squirm; it will destroy our bodies; it will hate us like it hated Christ. But we aren't without hope and we aren't without help.

I find the instructions Boaz gave Ruth intriguing. In them I see instructions for a foreigner in a new land, but I also see instructions for an ordinary outsider in a fallen world.

7. Review verses 8 and 9 of Ruth chapter 2. See if you can spot the five imperatives given to Ruth (put them in your own words).

Stay in My Field

Ruth was told to stay in Boaz's field for one very obvious reason: he would make sure she was provided for. A few verses later, he would instruct his reapers to make sure Ruth received enough grain to feed herself and her mother-in-law.

Doesn't the Lord ask the same of believers? He asks us to reap right where He has placed us. He asks us to move only when He leads us to move and to stay when He leads us to stay. In His field and in His will is where He provides. He invites us to glean in the field of His abundant grace. Anywhere outside of His will or His way leaves us vulnerable or condemned.

Stay Close

Boaz knew how hard it would be for a young woman like Ruth to carry her burden alone, so his provisions for her included the community of like women. Sure, Ruth had Naomi to guide her and teach her, but there would be things that Naomi would be unable to show her because of her age and limitations. So Boaz, in his wisdom, admonished Ruth to follow closely to the women (Ruth 2:8). More specifically they were the women in his field. These women wouldn't have been just anyone; they would have been women Boaz trusted and, therefore, who could lead Ruth by example in how to glean, prepare, and work.

As we discussed in lesson 3, the Christian life is not meant to be lived alone in anonymity without example or accountability. Like Ruth, we need like-minded women of all ages around us. The church in Acts knew this well. Acts 2:46–47 speaks of a church so alike in spirit that the believers met daily, ate together, and shared in one another's needs. Because of this they were joyful and their example drew many unbelievers to the church, and they, too, were saved.

8. Do you know anyone who can mentor you? Are you mentoring anyone?

Let Your Eyes Be on the Field

Boaz didn't want Ruth to get distracted. She had a job to do, one that would require her full attention. You see, there wouldn't always be a harvest. There would be an off-season and perhaps a lack of rain. So, while the fields were ready, Ruth needed to continue gleaning while the food was plentiful.

A couple of years ago my family and I were at the beginning of a long road full of big changes. It was there that the Lord gave me this phrase to hold on to: "my gaze transfixed on Jesus' face." It's from a song we often sing in church. Every time I hear it or repeat it to myself, I am reminded of where my focus should be. The things we went through were still difficult, more so than we had anticipated. But when we focused on God instead of on the hurdles ahead, we were able to see God's hand working and were able to persevere.

Go After Them

It was not enough for Ruth to keep her eyes on the field and follow the women, but she had to lend her hand to the work. Sure, Boaz was making provision for her by commanding the men to leave some grain behind on purpose (Ruth 2:16), but Ruth still had to put in the effort of collecting. The field needed to be both reaped and gleaned. The field wouldn't gather itself.

Oh, how this truth jumps out at me today! The many New Testament passages regarding a harvest have been ringing in my ears through the radio, my personal Bible study, the preaching in my home church, and the whispers of the Holy Spirit. In John 4:34–38 Jesus told His disciples, "Lift up your eyes and look at the fields, for they are already white for harvest!" Of course, Jesus wasn't speaking of grain, but of souls. There is work to do, and the harvest of souls is right now. We will either be watching the field of souls around us for opportunity to share Christ, or we will be useless tools that sit by while souls head straight for Hell.

9. Read Matthew 9:36–38. What is it that moved Jesus to ask His disciples to reap and to pray?

10. What did Jesus tell them to pray for?

When we go out into the field to harvest, to share Jesus and His offer of salvation, we have a great "cloud of witnesses" that have gone before us (Hebrews 12:1). Many of those witnesses are mentioned in Hebrews 11. We have footsteps to walk in, and we can "go after them" into the harvest because we have seen it done before through the examples in God's Word.

When You Are Thirsty, Drink

As Jesus had compassion, so we see Boaz showing compassion for Ruth's relational and physical needs (Ruth 2:9). By encouraging her to drink from the vessels drawn by the men, he was making sure another physical need was being met.

Jesus, too, provides drink for us, but in a totally different capacity. Yes, He cares about our physical needs, but His primary focus is on our great spiritual need. Jesus told the woman at the well in John 4 that the water in her well would provide only temporary physical relief but that what He had to offer was eternal spiritual relief—the salvation of her soul. One drink from the spring of Living Water, Who is Jesus, redeems our souls for eternity. And then we have full-time access to the Holy Spirit within us for our daily need.

The Prayer of Boaz

Boaz's tenderness and care for Ruth are beautifully exemplified in his prayer over her.

11. Write his prayer, found in Ruth 2:12.

It should be noted that Boaz, too, had action in his faith as he became the answer to his own prayers over Ruth, or at least the tool God used. First Boaz prayed that she be repaid for her work; then he immediately invited her to eat and made provision for her work to be prosperous and safe.

However, the second part of his prayer—that she be given a "full reward . . . by the LORD God of Israel"—he could not be the answer to. A full reward would be that the Lord God of Israel would recognize her faith as a saving faith. Boaz was reiterating her faith to her, recognizing it, and pointing her back to the Lord God, Who had called her out of Moab and under "whose wings" she sought refuge.

I Am Accepted

Ruth had been through the ringer, but look at what came flowing from her heart when she suddenly became the recipient of Boaz's grace and compassion.

12. Write out the things Ruth was thankful for in verses 10 and 13.

Ruth fell on her face and proclaimed, probably through tears, a prayer of thanksgiving. When Ruth used the word *favor* or *grace,* she was acknowledging the wonder of being found acceptable to Boaz. Likewise, we can be found acceptable to God when we fall before Him and let His extraordinary grace cover our sin through the perfect sacrifice of His Son, Jesus.

13. Write out Ephesians 1:6.

The reach of sin is total and all-encompassing. This means that we, even the most innocent among us, are still totally depraved (Romans 3:9–18). It is hard for me to look on the innocent face of my infant and think that sin lies deep in her heart and permeates every part of her being (Proverbs 22:15), but give it a few months and soon the deceit, selfishness, and greed will begin to show. The anger and hatred for authority will manifest in disobedience and screaming fits.

All My Harvest

Read Ruth 2:19–23.

Naomi was a bit overwhelmed when she heard Ruth recount her day, particularly when she heard the name Boaz. You can almost see the light bulb flash on above her head. This man was no ordinary farmer; he was a close kin and had bestowed his grace on the women abundantly. Naomi again recognized the sovereignty of God, this time through words of praise instead of lament, as she declared a blessing on "he of the LORD, who has not forsaken His kindness to the living and the dead" (Ruth 2:20).

But the hope forming in Naomi's mind required patience. Ruth had been invited to continue to glean until the end of all the harvests. While the barley harvest would have happened in April, the last harvest could be a few months later. So Naomi said no more about Boaz. Ruth settled into working, and Naomi settled into waiting.

Personal Application

What does this tell me about God?

Which of God's attributes is displayed in Ruth 2:1–23?

How can I apply this to my life?

A Floor

Ruth 3:1–18

IF YOU'RE ANYTHING LIKE ME, as you end your reading of Ruth 3, a big question may be on your mind: What did I just read? So Boaz is sleeping on the floor, Ruth sneaks in and lies down at his feet (which obviously scares the daylights out of him), then they say some stuff about a wing and a close relative, and we're all okay with this?

I'm with you. At first glance this looks a little bonkers. But this wouldn't be a Bible study if we had all the answers, now would it? What looks so strange is actually quite beautiful when considered in the context of the story and in the landscape of the culture.

The Story

More about the Harvest

Read Ruth 3:1–2.

Ever since Naomi heard the name Boaz back at the beginning of chapter 2, the possibility of a marriage proposal had been in the back of her mind. What a blessing of God's providence it was for Ruth to land in Boaz's field and then to find such favor in his eyes. Naomi surely never would have predicted it, but there it was, a tiny speck of hope. But the wise woman kept her wits and simply watched, waited, and prayed for the right moment throughout all the harvests.

In the meantime, Ruth did what we've come to expect Ruth to do. She continued to work and to glean. She continued to keep herself with propriety and virtue. It would seem that Ruth had no idea of the possibility that lurked in the distance. If she did, she didn't act the way most young women probably would, strutting around seeking attention. She was meek and faithful.

When chapter 3 opens, we hear Naomi express her desire to seek security, or rest, for Ruth. Boaz, she thinks, is the answer. He could provide a physical rest, so that Ruth would no longer need to glean. And Naomi knew exactly where to find him.

1. Where did Naomi say Boaz would be and what would he be doing?

Gathering a harvest is a laborious three-step process. First there is reaping, or in Ruth's case gleaning. Reaping is an intense task of gathering the stalks of grain from where they grow in the field. In Ruth's day, this was done by either pulling the stalks up by the roots or cutting them with a sickle. The stalks would then be tied together and brought by bundles to the threshing floor for threshing.

2. In Ruth's time, gleaning would have been a menial task—a provision for the poor and needy. It also would have been a humbling task. What might be a modern equivalent?

Second, there is threshing, the process used to remove the grains from the stalks. Sometimes basic machinery is used, but likely in Ruth's case, she would have beaten the stalks against the ground. The heads of grain would fall off the stalks, and the stalks would be discarded or used for the care and feeding of animals.

The final process is called winnowing. During a good

threshing, the grain falls from the stalks, but so does undesirable particles called chaff. In Ruth's day, this would most likely be the husks that had surrounded the grain. While it was possible to separate the chaff from the grain by hand, it would be very time-consuming. Because the grains were heavier than the chaff, the worker would stand on a stool or a large stone, lift a bowl filled with the grain and chaff mixture high overhead, and slowly pour it out onto the ground. The breeze would do the work of carrying the chaff away, while the grain fell to a cloak or piece of fabric on the ground.

Two Laws

Before we go any further, it's important to understand two Israelite laws: the law of redemption and the law of levirate marriage.

The law of redemption is found in Leviticus 25:23–28. This law made allowances for a land owner who had come into some financial trouble to sell his land to his closest kin. The closest kin would purchase the land, keep it running, and then would return the land to the original owner at the year of Jubilee. The year of Jubilee occurred every fifty years. All the slaves were set free, all the sold properties were returned to the original owners, and there was no reaping or sowing (Leviticus 25). It was an entire year of freedom, rest, and worship.

The law of levirate marriage is found in Deuteronomy 25:5–10. This law provided that if a woman's husband died without producing an heir and the deceased husband had a brother who was unmarried, then the surviving brother would marry his sister-in-law. He would then care for the widow as his wife. The children, or at least the firstborn son, produced from the second union would be heirs to the deceased man's property and would carry on his name. This addressed a couple of issues, ensuring the widow would be cared for, property would not go on without someone to inherit it, and the dead man's legacy would live on.

It certainly sounds like Boaz was set up to be the answer to Naomi's prayers for Ruth (Ruth 1:9), but both laws mention that the requirement for fulfilling the law fell on a closest kinsman (redeeming relative) or the husband's brother.

3. According to Ruth 2:20 and 3:12, did Boaz meet the requirements? Why or why not?

It is no surprise that Boaz didn't step up to redeem the land or marry Ruth on his own. He was not another of Naomi's sons, and he was only one of the close relatives, not the closest. Although marrying Ruth was not something Boaz was required to do, it was still something he could do.

4. Why do you think Boaz didn't pursue a marriage to Ruth on his own?

A Goel

While Boaz might not have met the requirements for the two laws already mentioned, under the right circumstances he was certainly *capable* of performing the act of a goel. To the ancient Israelites, a goel was a close relative who would step up to buy back lands sold during times of poverty, buy back relatives who were sold into slavery, avenge the blood of a murdered relative, fulfill the law of redemption, and on some occasions step in to perform fulfillment of levirate marriage by marrying a widow who had no heir.

The Hebrew word *goel* is derived from another term (*gaul*) meaning "to redeem." Therefore, the word *goel* means "redeemer." The goel is one who redeems, purchases, sets right, and avenges, giving the Israelites a physical representation of the all-important concept of redemption.

The goel wasn't just anyone, but was someone close of kin, someone of the same line, someone who knew well the person or property he was redeeming. Our English theologians and scholars have often used the term *kinsman-redeemer* to describe more fully what a goel would mean to the Israelites, thereby better describing what Boaz would mean to Ruth.

Naomi's Instructions

Read Ruth 3:3–5.

With so much hanging on the line, Naomi wasn't taking any chances. She gave Ruth six instructions. We can sum up the instructions like this: wash, anoint, dress, go, watch, and wait. And, of course, in true Ruth fashion, she listened.

Wash, Anoint, and Dress

5. Why do you think Naomi told Ruth to wash and anoint herself?

Ruth and Naomi were in hard times. Ruth had spent most of her time—probably all of her daylight hours—gleaning in the field. It was smelly, dirty work. So Naomi's instructions to wash and anoint could have been as simple as "clean up and smell nice."

Ruth was also told to put on her best clothes. The meaning is kind of ambiguous. It could have been an instruction to simply continue making herself look her very best. However, considering that Ruth had lost her husband not long before, Naomi could have been telling her to do something much more profound.

In 2 Samuel we see a passage that tells about a woman who was asked to pretend to be a mourner. It says, "And Joab sent to Tekoa and brought from there a wise woman, and said to her, 'Please pretend to be a mourner, and put on mourning apparel; do not anoint yourself with oil, but act like a woman who has been mourning a long time for the dead'" (2 Samuel 14:2).

6. What was the woman in 2 Samuel 14 told to do to make herself look like a mourner?

Mourning the death of a close relative, such as a husband, would have meant that Ruth would have worn mourning clothes for an extended period and refrained from perfuming herself with oil. It is possible that when Naomi instructed Ruth to wash, anoint, and put on her best clothes, she was telling Ruth that her time of mourning had ended and a time for rejoicing was coming.

Go, Watch, and Wait

Read Ruth 3:5–9.

But first Ruth had to go to the threshing floor in secret, watch where Boaz lay, uncover his feet, lie down, and wait.

7. What was Ruth's response to Naomi's strange request?

The amount of faith and trust it took for Ruth to obey Naomi must have been tremendous. I can imagine myself responding quite differently. Sure, Boaz was an appealing prospect, but wasn't there a better way? Maybe during the daytime? And why uncover his feet? So many questions would have spilled out of my mouth. But Ruth, thankfully, was not like I am and obeyed without questioning.

8. I like to call this "faith with feet on it." Have you ever stepped out in this kind of faith and done something that seemed crazy at the time, but you knew God was in it? Or have you ever not done something you knew God wanted you to because it was uncomfortable, and perhaps you missed a blessing?

This being the tail end of the harvest, the threshing floor probably had a lively and celebratory atmosphere. Verse 7 of chapter 3 says that when Boaz had "eaten and drunk, and his heart was cheerful, he went to lie down at the end of the heap of grain."

9. Why do you think his heart was cheerful?

It is likely that Boaz would have lain down near the grain to protect it from thieves and to be ready for another day of work when the sun rose. He would have slept with a merry heart, because after ten years, the famine had finally come to an end, thanks to the rescue by the Lord. Boaz had the distinct privilege of seeing suffering and oppression yield to a harvest of abundance.

The threshing floor was likely out of doors, providing him with a stunning view of the stars overhead. What a moment to reflect on all that Jehovah had done for His people. Even though wisdom told Boaz to guard his grain in case the oppressors came again, he was able to close his eyes with gladness and rejoicing in his heart.

When the moment came that his eyes finally closed in deep sleep, Ruth went to him, uncovered his feet, and took her position just as she had been told. He slept. She did not. And when he was startled, he could sense that someone was with him.

10. When Boaz asked who was there, how did Ruth respond?

11. This was not the first time that Ruth had called herself a
    "maidservant." What was the other time? Why did she refer
    to herself with this word? Hint: look in lesson 4.

A Shocking Request

Read Ruth 3:9–18.

While what has preceded was Ruth responding in obedience to Naomi's instructions, what follows is a glimpse at Ruth's
spunk. Naomi's instructions were just to listen, and Boaz would
tell Ruth what to do. Instead she spoke up, making a shocking
request.

12. What did she say to Boaz?

If you recall, back when the two first met, Boaz commended
Ruth for her work and for her faith to go to the "LORD God of Is-
rael, under whose wings [she had] come for refuge" (Ruth 2:12).
And Ruth used his own words.

13. Based on what you have learned, what did Ruth's request
    mean?

Again Boaz had the opportunity to be the answer to his own
prayers through the providential work of Almighty God. You
can almost hear the shock and surprise in his voice when he

responded saying, "Blessed are you of the LORD, my daughter! For you have shown more kindness at the end than at the beginning, in that you did not go after young men, whether poor or rich" (Ruth 3:10).

14. In what ways do you see Ruth's second kindness as being better than the first, as Boaz said?

Ruth's second kindness was truly better than the first. She was presenting herself to someone who could provide not only for her but also for her mother-in-law, and who could continue the legacy of Elimelech, her deceased father-in-law, and her first husband, Mahlon.

You know what I love best about Boaz's response? Okay, there are three things.

First, I love that Boaz had such affection for Ruth. He called her "my daughter" and a "virtuous woman." He also encouraged her to "not fear" (Ruth 3:11). His love for her was evident, hinting that he had been an admirer from the moment he saw her in his field.

Second, I love that he guarded her purity and her reputation by encouraging her to lie at his feet until morning—and even more so when he sent her back to Naomi with a load of barley before the sun was bright enough for her face to be seen (Ruth 3:14–15).

Third, I love that he already knew exactly who the closer relative was, where to find him, and when. I believe that Boaz had already thought about performing the role of the goel but that for some reason, he had not followed through. He had, however, played the idea in his mind enough that he knew exactly whom he needed to talk to and how to find him.

15. Based on this interaction (Ruth 3:9–15), what can we learn
    of Boaz's character?

The Gospel

The threshing floor was where the grain was separated from
the stalks and the chaff from the grain. This is where Ruth found
Boaz, her kinsman-redeemer. The same place that Boaz gathered his wheat into the barn was the same place that Ruth asked
to be gathered under his wings.

People in a largely agricultural community like the ones in
ancient Israel would have understood the necessity of the grain
compared to the waste of the chaff. Their physical lives de-
pended on it. The Bible is full of parables and metaphors that
use a harvest, its grain, and the chaff to represent the kingdom of God and the eternal destination of believers versus
nonbelievers.

Psalm 1:4 says, "The ungodly . . . are like the chaff which
the wind drives away." While Matthew 13:30 says, "I [the Lord]
will say to the reapers, . . . 'Gather the wheat into my barn.'"
The wheat, a precious commodity to Ruth then—and still to us
today—was gathered carefully and protected. It was the beautiful result of a careful master to sow and to reap. The wheat was
gathered into the barn to be a part of the master's celebration.

16. According to Matthew 3:12, what happens to the chaff?

17. According to Matthew 13:49–50, who is the chaff?

The Bible leaves no room for error. The wheat are those who believe and follow Christ; the chaff are the ungodly who don't believe and who serve their own sinful lusts (1 John 2:15–17). The unbeliever will experience eternal punishment in fire. The believer will be gathered with the Lord in Heaven for eternal celebration and praise.

Seeking Security

Ruth had been striving to provide for Naomi and herself. After months of this, Naomi decided the time had come for Ruth's striving to end. Naomi told Ruth she wanted to seek security for her (Ruth 3:1). The word *security* in verse 1 of chapter 3 may also be translated "rest." Security and rest were the two things that Ruth needed. Boaz was very likely to be the answer to those needs.

Security and rest are needs we all have from the moment we are born; however it's our souls, not our bodies, that are the most desperate for it. This is why Jesus said in Matthew 11:29–30 to take on His yoke and burden because they are "easy" and "light" and He will give us "rest." All our striving after righteousness and security is useless before God.

He is a holy God Who requires justice. Amazingly, He is also a loving God Who gave grace when He allowed His Son to take the just punishment we deserve. Christ wants to take our filth and redeem it with His richness, to replace our shame and redeem it with His glory. This is the power of our goel, the true Kinsman-Redeemer, Jesus Christ.

In surrender, Ruth placed herself at Boaz's feet. It was akin to bowing in submission, coming to the altar, or falling at Jesus' feet. Numerous times in the Gospels we get to see men and women surrendering themselves at the feet of Jesus in a similar fashion.

18. In the following passages, note what the people were seeking or doing when they laid themselves at Jesus' feet.

Matthew 15:30

Mark 7:25

Luke 17:16

John 11:32–33

As Ruth laid herself at Boaz's feet, she had nothing with her. She had nothing to give to entice Boaz into making such a risky move like marrying a Moabite woman and taking on her burden. She went, knowing he didn't need her, that she needed him.

When we come to the feet of Jesus, we bring nothing with us. There is nothing we have that we can give to God that would make Him better or stronger or more important. He is all-sufficient. This means He needs nothing from anyone. He has it all. Nothing lacking. When we surrender ourselves to Him, both when we seek His forgiveness through salvation and when we seek His help daily, there is nothing we can bring to sweeten the deal.

Yet He still wants us to come to Him, to His feet. I can't explain why He would want someone like me—someone who is way too flawed to warrant such extravagant love—but still He reaches down and pursues me. He seeks each of us to redeem us and to claim us as His own. He wants to buy us back from slavery to sin and then to bind us to Him forever.

Be Still

When Ruth returned to Naomi, she didn't yet know how it would turn out. She knew Boaz was going to pursue the deal,

but she didn't know how the closer kinsman would respond. Naomi, in her wisdom, led Ruth with one final instruction.
19. In Ruth 3:18, what did Naomi tell Ruth to do?

Stillness is not something many of us are very good at, my-self included. I love the feeling of being in motion, of checking things off of my to-do list, and of tackling challenges head-on (sometimes with an unfortunate dose of recklessness).

But sitting still is sometimes all God calls us to do. In Exodus 14, the Israelites had just been released from Egypt when Pha-raoh changed his mind and pursued them. The Israelites were facing the sea in front, and the chariots of Egypt were closing in behind. The Israelites were terrified. In their fear, they begin to complain and cry out, but Moses instructed them in wisdom.
20. Look up Exodus 14:13–14. What was his response?

The altar is always open. The arms of the Father are always waiting. Your rest has already been secured. Freedom and for-giveness have already been bought. Fall at His feet and be still.

Personal Application

What does this tell me about God?

Which of God's attributes is displayed in this passage?

How can I apply this to my life?

A Family

Ruth 4:1–22

AS WE BEGIN RUTH 4, we are at the great climax of our story. We know something is about to happen. We feel the suspense mounting as we wait to see how Boaz will handle the matter at hand. Thankfully, we don't have to wait long.

Boaz, the Kinsman-Redeemer

Read Ruth 4:1–12.

A man of integrity and true to his word, Boaz acted immediately and positioned himself at the city gate, where he knew the nearer kinsman would soon arrive. When he did, the two discussed the right to redeem Elimelech's property, while ten elders acted as witnesses. At first, the nearer kinsman said he would perform the goel function and redeem the land.

In an impressive negotiating move, however, Boaz performed a bait-and-switch possibly meant to scare the other man off. The man agreed to redeem the land only. He seemed to know nothing of the woman, Ruth, who would be included in the deal. When this was revealed, the man admitted that he couldn't perform the role, and he yielded the right of redemption to Boaz.

To be a kinsman-redeemer, Boaz had two boxes to check. First, he had to be a kinsman and the closest one willing and able to be a goel. Second, he had to perform the function and redeem Ruth as he had promised. He was already willing, but he had to get the other, closer relative to give up his first right.

The city gate was where legal transactions like this one would normally take place, and Boaz wasted no time in assembling a group of elders there, as would be required. When the other kinsman came by, Boaz pulled him into negotiations with a nod of kinship, calling him "friend" (Ruth 4:1).

As we know, the other kinsman at first was ready to redeem the land (Ruth 4:3–4). Perhaps adding the profit of Elimelech's property to his own would yield a good harvest for him in the years to come. Perhaps he understood the importance of the goel's role and, as a man of integrity himself, saw no reason why he shouldn't do it. In fact, it seemed that the other kinsman was about to ruin Boaz's plans.

1. What made the other kinsman refuse to redeem the land?

When the other kinsman realized that in order to redeem the land he would also be required to marry Ruth and care for her, he said, "I cannot redeem it for myself, lest I ruin my own inheritance" (Ruth 4:6). It is possible that the man was already married or that he simply didn't want the financial burden of a wife. Or possibly he didn't want to taint his inheritance with a Moabite woman. After all, Boaz was clever enough to make sure the other man knew that the woman was a foreigner.

It is unclear what it was about Ruth that would have ruined the nearer kinsman's own inheritance, but we do know that Boaz saw the situation quite differently. To the other kinsman, the price of redeeming the land was too high. But for Boaz, the deal was about more than an inheritance or his personal gain. He loved Ruth. The price of delivering her was well worth the cost or any personal loss he might incur.

2. Are there people in your life who don't seem worth it to you? Does seeing them as people that Jesus died to redeem help you see them differently?

Right there Boaz turned to the elders and to all the witnesses who had gathered and announced that he would redeem the property and deliver the woman, Ruth.

3. At the end of verse 10, Boaz gave a reason for his purchase. What was it?

From Foreigner to Family

Read Ruth 4:13–22.

It seems that Boaz didn't waste any time in making Ruth his wife. A marriage took place pretty quickly, and Ruth went from foreigner and maidservant to family member and wife.

4. Reflect for a moment. How does this movement from foreigner to family help you see God's ability to redeem your past?

God, also, didn't waste any time in blessing the two with a son. Interestingly, the women of the town were the ones to name the boy. Obed, they called him, meaning "servant." As Ruth had served Naomi and Boaz had served Ruth, the boy was being branded with the hope that he, too, would be a servant to the needs of others.

5. In Ruth 1 we saw Naomi desperately trying to convince Ruth
   to leave her. Together we noted that in her argument, Naomi
   used three desires: for home, for security of a husband and
   family, and for comfort of the familiar. In what ways has
   Ruth 4 addressed all of these desires?

The people of Bethlehem took pleasure in pouring out blessings over Boaz and Ruth. But Naomi, their dear friend whom
they had watched go from blessing to suffering and back again,
was certainly not forgotten in their prayers.

6. What did they pray for Naomi?

Naomi's original losses were not restored to her, but she was
given a grandson to carry on the inheritance of her husband and
a daughter-in-law who loved her and who was "better . . . than
seven sons" (Ruth 4:15).

7. According to verses 21 and 22, who was Ruth's
   great-grandson?

The second king of Israel was David, a shepherd boy from
Bethlehem, the great-grandson of a Moabite widow. Never
would Ruth have dreamed of such a legacy. When she watched
her first husband die, surely she never imagined that she would
have a descendant who would one day be the king of Israel. She
certainly couldn't have planned to have her story be a part of the
cannon of Scripture and her name remembered forever. And at
her death she couldn't have known what was to come from the
line of the son she bore.

8. According to Matthew 1:5 and 16, besides David, who else
   descended from Ruth and Boaz?

Miraculously and by the power of God's providence, from
the descendants of Ruth's marriage to Boaz came the true Redeemer. From the heart of Bethlehem came the Bread of Life.
From the line of the prostitute Rahab and then from the womb
of a pagan, Ruth, came the King of Kings.

Jesus Christ, the True and Better Redeemer

Everywhere you turn, whether in Ruth or anywhere else in
the Old Testament, the weight of redemption pulses through
each page. Redemption and deliverance were not just religious
ideas, but they were also real practices that bore out in the Israelites' everyday lives.

In such light, Boaz was being called upon to fulfill the role of
the kinsman-redeemer. But he was merely a man. While being a
kinsman redeemer showcased his virtue, compassion, love, and
wisdom, he was still a man with flaws and hang-ups. He could
redeem Ruth on earth, but her true redeemer, our Redeemer, is
far better.

9. In verse 10, Boaz said he was redeeming Ruth so that the
   "name of the dead may not be cut off." Reflect on this and
   share how you see Christ also fulfilling this role completely.

The true and better Redeemer would arrive in the same
town Ruth resided in. He would purchase her, not with money,
but with His precious blood. He would deliver her, not to secure
her immediate future from the despair of poverty, but to secure

an eternal one free from the carnage of sin. He would do so, not because she was a virtuous woman deserving of such, but because she was helplessly bound to sin and had no righteousness within her (Romans 3:10).

But redemption wasn't just for Ruth. Ephesians 1:7 says, "In Him we have redemption through His blood, the forgiveness of sins, according to the riches of His grace." We have redemption and forgiveness because of God's extraordinary grace. Boaz was a great redeemer for Ruth. But Christ is the true and better Redeemer for the whole world.

As the true and better Kinsman-Redeemer, Christ also had to be a kinsman. To redeem us, He had to become like us. He condescended to come to earth, leaving His glorious station in Heaven, and became fully Man while also being fully God. Once He was one of us, He had to suffer like one of us, yet without sin. He paid a high price and carried our sin in His agony on the cross.

10. In light of Ruth's redemption and its foreshadowing of the redemption provided by Christ, has the way you've seen your own story of redemption changed? How so?

11. For personal reflection, read the account of Jesus' crucifixion in John 19. Keep in mind that this is about the Redeemer and the price He paid for you. Write any thoughts below.

Can we imagine, for a moment, each of our own sins as a blow that struck His body? With each breath on the cross, He breathed in the stench of our depravity. With each mocking cry from the crowd, the wrath of our just God was poured out on His own Son so that we would not have to feel the darkness and pain of eternal damnation. What a high price we have on our heads.

But it was a price that He was willing and able to pay. It wasn't too high for Him. He wasn't worried about it ruining His inheritance. Jesus told one of the disciples in the moment the Roman guards came to take Him away that He could "pray to My Father, and He will provide Me with more than twelve legions of angels" (Matthew 26:53). Jesus was not forced to redeem us; He came and gave Himself willingly. He considered the cost and deemed us worthy of being redeemed.

Those who believe and put their faith in Christ immediately become a part of God's family, just as Ruth immediately became a part of Boaz's family. In 2 Corinthians 11 the church—the collection of believers, past, present, and future—is likened to the Bride of Christ. Elsewhere, for example in 1 John, believers are also called the children of God.

12. Look up 1 John 3:1. This passage says that it is by love that we believers are called children of God. But how did we get such a status?

For something to be bestowed, it must be owned by the giver first. Then it must be given freely to the recipient. Jesus Christ, the Son of God, is holy and completely righteous. He bestows His righteousness upon us to redeem us from the punishment we deserve. We don't earn redemption. It is a gift freely given (Romans 6:23).

13. How do you see the prayer of the women in Ruth 4:15 fulfilled in Jesus?

Jesus gives sinners new life, and by doing this, He answers the prayers that the women of Bethlehem offered on behalf of Naomi that her grandson be "to you a restorer of life and a nourisher of your old age." Obed would not and David would not. But Christ, the Son Who follows in this line, would truly be a "restorer of life" and a "nourisher" of all those who come to Him.

From the lineage of Ruth, a poor Moabite woman, and from the lineage of Rahab, a Canaanite prostitute, came our Kinsman-Redeemer. The genealogies in Scripture aren't there to bore us! They are there to point us to our Savior and to highlight that even in the ordinary, the common, and the foreign, He brings Himself glory.

The reality is that the Bible is not about us. This is not a story of our redemption; it is a story of our Redeemer. But, thankfully, we get to be a part of the story. The little moments that flash by every day, all the decisions we tackle, even every breath we take—all of it is orchestrated and used by our Heavenly Father. Nothing escapes His notice or care.

The Gospel

One reason this simple, heartwarming story is shared with us in the Word of God is because it points to a Savior. We are all poor foreigners, cut off from our Heavenly Father by our sin.

In fact, I need my Redeemer every day. Every single day I drop the ball. Nearly every night, when I crawl exhausted under the covers, I am moved to tears over the ways I have failed my children, my husband, and my God. I am not patient enough. I am not kind enough. I don't live out enough joy. I am not forgiving enough. I am not selfless enough. The Redeemer has rescued me from eternal damnation, but He also rescues me from me.

Boaz was a close kin by birth; Christ was a close kin by the power of His incarnation. Boaz, as the kinsman-redeemer, rescued the poor and lonely from poverty and obscurity, while

Christ, as the true and better Redeemer, rescued the bound from their sin.

Boaz walked to the city gate because that is where legal transactions would take place. His plan was to redeem one piece of land and one woman. Christ went to the cross because only there could justice be served and grace be poured out. His plan was to redeem all who would believe and restore creation at His second coming.

Boaz bought Ruth's deliverance by the power of human bargaining and with human resources. Christ secured our deliverance through the divine sacrifice of His death and the power of His resurrection.

Ruth's life was forever changed. She no longer needed to fear poverty or loneliness. Similarly, we are redeemed for life and for all eternity. As believers, we no longer need to fear spiritual death, poverty, or separation from God. We are forever united to Him through the gift of the Holy Spirit, never to walk alone.

Boaz claimed Ruth as his bride and in so doing transferred her from foreigner to family. Christ claims believers as His Bride, the church (2 Corinthians 11:2). By this we go from enemies of God to prized children of the Most High (Romans 5:10; Galatians 4:6).

I need the better Kinsman-Redeemer because I am weak and poor. He paid my debt on the cross, and every day He covers me in His grace and forgiveness. I need the Bridegroom Who rescues me from myself and binds me to Himself, making me an heir of His grace and a beneficiary of His Kingdom (Matthew 25:1–13).

It was our sin—my sin—that nailed Him to the cross. But it was because of His love for me that He willingly died. He knew all the sinful thoughts and all the wicked deeds that I would do. He knew that I would deny Him in my heart and turn away when He first called me. He knew that I would continue to struggle with pride, bitterness, and greed.

And still He came. And still He died. We are nothing special. We are all foreigners, outcasts, and sinners by birth. We are all ordinary. But we are also loved abundantly. He wants to make you family, to bring you under His wings, and make you His. Because of His love and by His extraordinary grace, you can be redeemed!

Application Questions

What does this tell me about God?

Which of God's attributes is displayed in this passage?

How can I apply this to my life?

Leader's Guide

Suggestions for Leaders

The effectiveness of a group Bible study usually depends on the leader and the ladies' commitment to prepare beforehand and interact during the study. You cannot totally control the second factor, but you have total control over the first one. These brief suggestions will help you be an effective Bible study leader.

Prepare each lesson a week in advance. During the week, read supplemental material and look for illustrations in the everyday events of your life and in the lives of others.

Encourage the ladies to complete each lesson before the meeting itself. This preparation will make the discussion more interesting.

The physical setting in which you meet will have some bearing on the study itself. Choose an informal setting that will encourage women to relax and participate. In addition to an informal setting, create an atmosphere in which ladies feel free to participate and be themselves.

During the discussion time, here are a few things to observe.

- Don't do all the talking. This study is not designed to be a lecture.
- Encourage discussion on each question by adding ideas and questions.
- Don't discuss controversial issues that will divide the group. (Differences of opinion are healthy; divisions are not.)
- Don't allow one lady to dominate the discussion. Use statements such as these to draw others into the study: "Let's hear from someone on this side of the room" (the side opposite the dominant talker); "Let's hear from someone who has not shared yet today."
- Stay on the subject. The tendency toward tangents is always possible in a discussion. One of your responsibilities as the leader is to keep the group on track.
- Don't get bogged down on a question that interests only one person.
- When there is no right or wrong answer to a question, the answer key says, "Personal answers." This doesn't mean that the question cannot be answered aloud, just that the question will be answered from a personal perspective. Feel free to invite ladies to respond aloud if they desire. But keep in mind the points listed above to keep your discussion uplifting and on track.

You may want to use the last fifteen minutes of the scheduled time for prayer. If you have a large group of ladies, divide into smaller groups for prayer. You could call this the "Share and Care Time."

If you have a morning Bible study, encourage the ladies to go out for lunch with someone else from time to time. This is a good way to get acquainted with new ladies. Occasionally you could plan a time when ladies bring their own lunches or salads to share and eat together. These things help promote fellowship and friendship in the group.

The formats that follow are suggestions only. You can plan your own format, use one of these, or adapt one of these to your needs.

2-hour Bible Study

10:00—10:15	Coffee and fellowship time
10:15—10:30	Get-acquainted time
	Have two ladies take five minutes each to tell something about themselves and their families.
	Also use this time to make announcements and, if appropriate, take an offering for the babysitters.
10:30—11:45	Bible study
	Leader guides discussion of the questions in the day's lesson.
11:45—12:00	Prayer time

2-hour Bible Study

10:00—10:45	Bible lesson
	Leader teaches a lesson on the content of the material. No discussion during this time.
10:45—11:00	Coffee and fellowship
11:00—11:45	Discussion time
	Divide into small groups with an appointed leader for each group. Discuss the questions in the day's lesson.
11:45—12:00	Prayer time

1½-hour Bible Study

10:00—10:30	Bible study
	Leader guides discussion of half the questions in the day's lesson.
10:30—10:45	Coffee and fellowship
10:45—11:15	Bible study
	Leader continues discussion of the questions in the day's lesson.
11:15—11:30	Prayer time

Answers

LESSON 1

1. In the days when the judges ruled.
2. *Joshua 24:23*—Put away the foreign gods and incline their hearts to the Lord (YHWH). *Deuteronomy 20:17–18*—Destroy the Hittites, Amorites, Canaanites, Perizzites, Hivites, and Jebusites.
3. They did not drive them out. Instead the Israelites either settled in the land with them or made them slaves.
4. To fill them. To provide for them.
5. They followed their own hearts and walked in their own counsel.
6. Personal answers.
7. Personal answers.
8. This wasn't a natural famine due to drought or plague; it was a forced famine. The Midianites would surround the Israelite towns and fields and steal the food right from under the Israelites. The Israelites were forced to hide out in caves and dens in the mountains.
9. Famine is an extreme scarcity of food.
10. Possible answers: Desperation and perhaps lack of faith.
11. Personal answers.
12. Mahlon and Chilion.
13. Personal answers.
14. Personal answers. Faith is a firm belief or trust in something or someone.
15. Personal answers. The dictionary says trust is assured reliance on the character, ability, strength, or truth of someone or something.
16. Personal answers.
17. Rebellion or disobedience.
18. Possible answers: We don't want to be responsible. If we believe our sins affect only us, it is easier for us to hold on to them rather than surrender them to God and abandon them.
19. Personal answers.

Personal Application

About God—God is not removed from us. He sees us and cares about our needs. He also requires our submission to Him. He demands our worship and obedience.

God's attributes—God is immanent, involved in our everyday life.

Application—Personal answers. I can look for God in my everyday moments. I can give Him my wholehearted worship and adoration because I know He sees me. And I can seek His help when I find it hard to trust.

LESSON 2

1. "Then she arose with her daughters-in-law that she might return from the

country of Moab, for she had heard in the country of Moab that the LORD had visited His people by giving them bread" (Ruth 1:6).

2. Ten years.
3. Possible answers: The bodies of her sons and husband were in Moab. If she left but her daughters-in-law stayed in Moab, she would surely miss them.
4. Naomi asked the blessings of God on them (Ruth 1:8–9). Ruth and Orpah were affectionate and wept greatly over separating or the thought of separating. Ruth clung to her.
5. A home.
6. The houses of their mothers and the houses of their future husbands.
7. Security.
8. She was heartbroken that her daughters-in-law were suffering because of their association with her.
9. Comfort.
10. Her people, her gods, and her sister-in-law.
11. Personal answers.
12. [Write a copy of Ruth's statement, which is found on page 25.]
13. Possible answer: She was giving up all her old ways to embrace a new people and a new culture, which included the Lord, Whom she had come to love.
14. Possible answer: Because of Naomi's faithful representation and witness.
15. Personal answers.
16. Through our praise, prayers, generosity, integrity, and joy in all circumstances.
17. Complaining, worrying, greed, deceit, and fear of the future.
18. They were both very determined.
19. Possible answers: Turning from old ways, old practices, or embracing the gospel for the first time no matter what that may mean for your relationships, job, etc.

Personal Application

About God—God loves us all and is a friend to sinners. He wants a personal relationship with me. God cares about our personal relationships here on earth. And He can use these relationships to draw us closer to Him.

God's attributes—God is love in giving us a substitutionary sacrifice in His Son, Jesus.

Application—Personal answers. I can cultivate godly relationships that are centered on a mutual love of Christ. I can be more giving of myself to others who may need a friend or a shoulder to cry on. I can commit myself to Christ, confessing my sins and believe in His sacrifice to save me from the power and punishment of my sins.

LESSON 3

1. "Do not call me Naomi; call me Mara, for the Almighty has dealt very bitterly with me. I went out full, and the D has brought me home again empty. Why do you call me Naomi, since the LORD has testified against me, and the Almighty has afflicted me?"
2. Personal answers. Certainly, returning home in a much different state than when she had left, and with less company, was like salt in an already raw

wound, and it burned. The once-sweet Naomi, her name meaning "pleasant," is now asking to be called Mara.
3. Bitter.
4. The book of Job.
5. "I AM WHO I AM" or "I AM."
6. Personal answers.
7. Personal answers.

Personal Application

About God—God's ways are higher than our ways. He always has our good in mind when He allows and brings about things in our lives. It may not always be fun or comfortable, but it will always be good. And we can have hope that God will use us to bring Him glory.

God's attributes—His sovereignty, His goodness, and His omnipotence.

Application—Personal answers. I can trust God to handle my highs and my lows. I can trust Him to do what is good. I can trust Him with my rejoicing and with my lament.

LESSON 4

1. *Genesis 16:1, 7–10, 13*—Hagar was an Egyptian slave. God blessed her and told her she would also birth a mighty nation. *Luke 17:12–19*—The leper was a Samaritan. God healed and blessed his faith. *Joshua 2; 6:25*—Rahab was a Canaanite prostitute. God, through Joshua, protected her and welcomed her into the family of Israel.
2. Boaz invited Ruth to eat with him and his employees, to share their bread, and to "dip your piece of bread in the vinegar" (Ruth 2:14).
3. Possible answers: *Ruth 1:14*—Compassion. *Ruth 1:16–17*—Loyalty, commitment, selflessness. *Ruth 1:18*—Determination. *Ruth 2:2*—Humility, go-getter. *Ruth 2:7*—Perseverance. *Ruth 2:10*—Gratitude. *Ruth 2:17*—Hardworking. *Ruth 2:18*—Generosity. *Ruth 2:23*—Faithfulness/loyalty.
4. She was his mother. Some scholars say she was his grandmother. Either way the truth is the same.
5. She settled into Israel and was still there when the book of Joshua was written.
6. They were to let Ruth glean freely, even among the parts of the field that had not yet been reaped. In addition, they were to purposefully drop some of the grain they had reaped so she could easily gather it for herself.
7. (1) Do not go to glean in another field; don't go from here; (2) stay close; (3) let your eyes be on the field; (4) follow along with the women; (5) when you are thirsty, get a drink.
8. Personal answers.
9. Compassion. Jesus was moved with compassion for the multitudes because they were, like sheep without a shepherd, "weary and scattered."
10. To send laborers to the harvest.
11. "The LORD repay your work, and a full reward be given you by the LORD God of Israel, under whose wings you have come for refuge."
12. Boaz's comfort, kindness, and favor.

13. "To the praise of the glory of His grace, by which He made us accepted in the Beloved."

Personal Application

About God—He loves outcasts, foreigners, ordinary, poor, rich, and everyone in between. His desire, from the beginning, was that all would be saved.

God's attributes—God is merciful and immutable. His plan has always been to save us "foreigners" and "gentiles."

Application—Personal answers. Because God knows everything I don't, I can be faithful with what He has given me and follow where He leads. God is love. He loves all of us, no matter where we come from or what we've done.

LESSON 5

1. On the threshing floor, winnowing grain.
2. Personal answers.
3. No. According to Naomi's own words in Ruth 2:20, he was one of their "close relatives," not their closest, and he said the same thing (3:12).
4. Personal answers.
5. Personal answers.
6. To put on mourning apparel and to not anoint herself with oil.
7. She said, "All that you say to me I will do."
8. Personal answers.
9. Personal answers.
10. "I am Ruth, your maidservant."
11. Ruth called herself a maidservant in 2:13, when she met him in the field. She called herself this because she had taken on the role of a servant by working in his field. It was also a term of humility. She knew she was unworthy of his favor.
12. "Take your maidservant under your wing, for you are a close relative."
13. It was a marriage proposal. She was reminding him that he was a close relative and letting him know she wanted him to perform the duty of a goel.
14. Her second kindness meant that she wasn't pursuing what would necessarily fill a temporary thrill or comfort. She was looking down the road at what path would be most pleasing to her mother-in-law and to her new God. She was remembering the husband of her past by reaching out to a second potential husband who could make sure the first was not forgotten.
15. He was humble, righteous, kind, gentle, thoughtful, and generous.
16. It will be burned with unquenchable fire.
17. The wicked.
18. *Matthew 15:30*—seeking healing; *Mark 7:25*—seeking her daughter's freedom from possession by an evil spirit; *Luke 17:16*—giving thanks; *John 11:32–33*—weeping.
19. Sit still.
20. "Do not be afraid. Stand still, and see the salvation of the LORD, which He will accomplish for you today. . . . The LORD will fight for you, and you shall hold your peace."

Personal Application

About God—Salvation wasn't a secondary thought to God. He has planned for our redemption from the beginning and has been weaving it into the landscape of history from the start. He will fight and has fought for me. He does not need me, but He does want me.

God's attributes—God is just and holy. No sin or sinner can approach Him. But He is also merciful, providing a way for salvation. He is all-sufficient.

Application—I can fully surrender to Him because I am nothing without Him. I can do nothing without His help and His grace. I can lay down my striving and be still, knowing that He is fighting for me.

LESSON 6

1. If he redeemed the land, he also had to take Ruth as his wife (Ruth 4:5).
2. Personal answers.
3. "That the name of the dead may not be cut off from among his brethren and from his position at the gate."
4. Personal answers.
5. Ruth's desire for a home was satisfied in a marriage to Boaz. Her desire for security was satisfied in her marriage and the son the marriage produced. The son would carry on the legacy and care for Ruth in her old age. The desire for comfort was satisfied in the wonderful people of Bethlehem, who showered Ruth in affection and prayers of blessing.
6. That the son would be famous in Israel and that he would be a restorer of life and a nourisher to her in her old age.
7. David.
8. Jesus Christ.
9. Personal answers. In Christ, those who are dead in their sin are given new life (Luke 15:32; Ephesians 2:1). We are no longer cut off from our Heavenly Father and from our position in His family (John 1:12; Romans 8:1, 16–17).
10. Personal answers.
11. Personal answers.
12. It was bestowed on us.
13. Personal answers. He is the One Who gives life and nourishes believers' souls.

Personal Application

About God—He is the hero of the story; we are just the beneficiaries. He rescues and redeems.

God's attributes—Holy and just, requiring payment for sin. Love, to give Himself as that payment. Merciful, to allow us to be part of His family.

Application—I can remember every day that it is only by His power and by His grace I have another day in which to bring Him glory. I can act like a child of God by practicing His attributes of mercy, grace, and love. I can leave behind fear, knowing that He plans my way and that His way is very good.